P9-DFI-139

# Contents

**World Book, Inc.**
a Scott Fetzer company
Chicago

Property of Library

# Childcraft—The How and Why Library

**C**hildcraft—The How and Why Library brings you 15 wonderful new books. These books are packed with exciting things to read about and lots of activities to do and things to make.

Do you have one special interest? You will probably be able to read all about it in a volume of your **Childcraft** set. But if you look hard, you may find out things you never guessed in other volumes, too.

This booklet, **Fun with Childcraft**, challenges you to find out about nine exciting topics. It sets you off on a treasure hunt of

knowledge, dipping into every volume in search of new and amazing facts. Each topic will tell you how you can find the answers to all kinds of questions in your **Childcraft** set.

At the end of each topic, there is a short quiz. Find a pen and paper and see how many questions you can answer. If you have a brother, sister, or friend, try out some of the questions together!

**Fun with Childcraft** will send you on a fabulous voyage of discovery through your new **Childcraft** set.

# Hot and Cold

## Making things colder

◆ When you put warm food into a refrigerator, the food soon grows cold. Where has the heat from the food gone? Find out on **pages 16-17** of **How Things Work**.

## Going up!

◆ Have you ever seen a huge balloon floating in the sky? What keeps it up in the air? Find out on **pages 96-97** of **How Does It Happen?**

## Desert sands

◆ The sun beats down on a blanket of yellow sand. There are no green plants in sight. The air is so hot that it shimmers. This is what most people imagine when they think of a desert. But there are many different kinds of deserts. Look on **pages 64-67** of **Our Earth**.

## Making things hotter

### Disappearing ice

◆ Can you fry an ice cube? You can try, but the heat soon will melt the ice into water. Then the water will evaporate. Where does it go? Find out on **pages 88-89** of **How Does It Happen?**

### Storing the sun

◆ One day you may live in a house that is kept warm by the sun. Big panels will collect the heat of the sun. But how can you store it? See **pages 70-71** of **How Does It Happen?**

# Icy cold

◆ Where is the coldest place on earth? The answer is Antarctica, where a sheet of ice more than 1 mile (1.6 kilometers) thick covers the land. The air is so cold that the moisture in your breath freezes into tiny ice crystals. Do you know where Antarctica is? Look it up on **pages 20-21** of **See the World.**

## Br-r-r-r

◆ It's blowing, it's snowing. Read the poems about snow on **pages 37-39** of **Poems and Rhymes.**

# Getting around

## Skis and sleds

◆ Trudging through snow is hard work! Find out how people travel around in snowy places on **pages 42-43** of **See the World.**

## Across the sands

◆ It's easy for camels to walk on desert sand. **Page 49** of **See the World** tells you how they do this.

# Rivers of ice

◆ High in the mountains, the ice groans and cracks. It creeps slowly down the valley in a great frozen river called a glacier. Far out at sea, a massive iceberg drifts silently. How did it get there? Find out about glaciers and icebergs on **pages 70-71** of **Our Earth.**

## Mountains of fire

◆ Far down in the earth, it is so hot that the rocks have melted. Sometimes the molten rock pushes up out of the ground. It piles up into the shape of a cone and cools down. This is how a volcano is formed. There are thousands of volcanoes in the world. Read all about how they erupt on **pages 54-55** of **Our Earth.**

## Goosebumps and sweat

◆ When you are cold, do you get goosebumps on your skin? They appear when the tiny hairs on your body stand on end. The hairs trap a layer of warm air next to your skin to keep you warm. When you are hot, sweat comes out of your skin. As the sweat dries, you feel cooler. Find out why your skin is busy all the time on **pages 18-19** of **About You.**

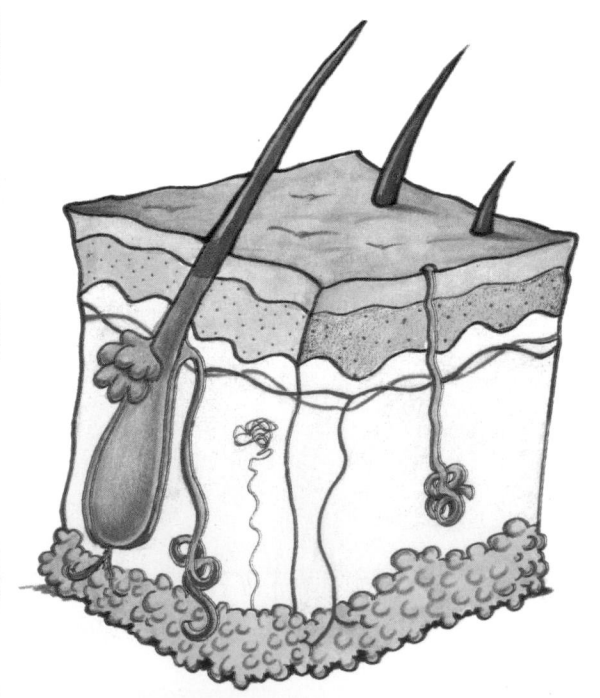

## Covering up

◆ One man lives in the icy Arctic. He wears thick, furry trousers, a hooded jacket, and a pair of sealskin boots. A woman lives in the hot climate of India. She wears a light flowing gown. In the hot Sahara Desert, another man wears loose robes that cover him from head to foot. Why do they wear such different clothes? Read **pages 72-75** of **See the World** and you will find out.

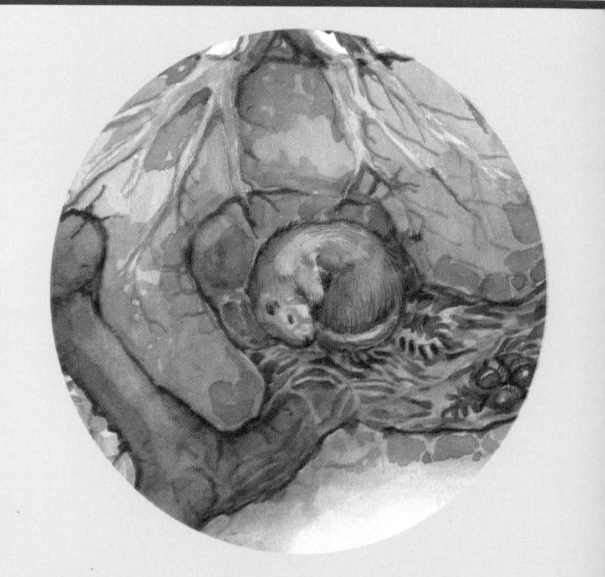

## A long winter sleep

◆ In the autumn, a woodchuck curls up into a ball and goes to sleep. Its heart beats slowly. Its body grows cold. All through the cold weather it stays asleep. It will wake up when the warm spring weather arrives. What do we call this kind of sleeping? Read **pages 158-159** of **The World of Animals** for the answer.

## Winter and summer

◆ Everyone knows that it is warm in the summer and cooler in the winter. But when it is summer in your part of the world, it is winter somewhere else. And there are places in the world where it is summery all year! Find out where on **pages 22-25** of **The Universe.**

## Desert and tundra plants

### A prickly customer

◆ In a desert, the ground is baked dry by the sun. But plants still need water. How has the cactus solved this problem? Find out on **pages 76-79** of **The World of Plants.**

## Plants on ice

◆ Winters are fiercely cold, dark, and long. So tundra plants need to do all their growing during the few short months of summer. Get to know some of these hardy plants on **pages 80-83** of **The World of Plants.**

## How much heat?

◆ What do you reach for when you want to measure the amount of heat in something? A thermometer, of course. **Pages 14-15** of **How Things Work** introduce you to several kinds of thermometers.

## Hot and cold quiz

Here are some questions about hot and cold. Try to think of the answers. Then turn to the pages listed to find the answers.

◆ What is lava? **volume 6, page 54**

◆ What do molecules do when they are hot? **volume 8, page 88**

◆ Why do caribou migrate south in winter? **volume 4, page 160**

◆ What happens to clay when it is baked in a very hot oven? **volume 3, page 80**

# All About Plants

## Hitchhikers and exploders

◆ Plants need to scatter their seeds to grow new plants. Some hitch a ride or fly or float. Other seed pods explode! Find out how seeds travel on **pages 22-23** of **The World of Plants.**

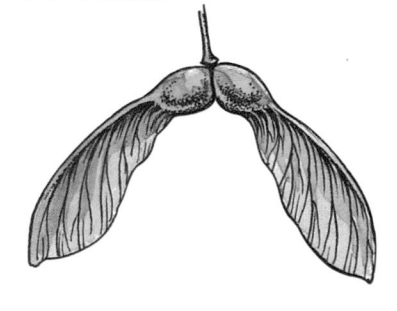

## Products from plants

### Clothes

◆ Some plants can be made into cloth to make clothes. Are you wearing plants today? Find out on **pages 134-135** of **How Things Work** and **108-109** of **The World of Plants.**

## Buildings

◆ If you lived in a forest, you might use wood from the trees to build your house. If you lived near a lake, you might use reeds. Villagers in the African bush build their homes from bamboo. See some pictures of homes made of plants on **pages 106-107** of **The World of Plants.**

## Tires and tennis shoes

◆ Next time you put on your tennies and jump on your bicycle or into a car, thank the rubber tree. The rubber in tires and tennis shoes is made from the juice of this tree. **Pages 108-109** of **The World of Plants** describe how it is done.

## Paper

◆ How does a tall tree become thin sheets of paper? Read about the journey from logs to paper on **pages 126-127** of **How Things Work.**

## Tasty plants

◆ When a British mother says to her children, "Eat your vegetables," she may mean cabbage, carrots, or potatoes. But in other parts of the world, the vegetables on the plate may be mustard leaves, bean sprouts, or olives. Find out on **pages 52-53** of **Who We Are** where these vegetables come from.

## What's inside a leaf?

◆ Leaves don't seem to do anything at all. But if you were tiny enough to look inside a leaf, you would have quite a surprise! What would you find? **Pages 18-19** of **The World of Plants** will show you.

## Unusual Features

### The stinker

◆ The rafflesia is the largest flower in the world. It is also the smelliest. Why is it good for it to be so stinky, and how big does it get? **Page 166** of **The World of Plants** explains.

### The dodder

◆ The dodder wraps itself around another plant and sucks out all the plant's food and water. But the dodder is not the only plant that's a thief. Read about another on **page 47** of **The World of Plants.**

### The insect trappers

◆ Deep in the swamp lives a strange plant whose leaves are a death trap. Spines like claws grow from the edges of its folded leaves. When an insect lands on a leaf, the two halves snap shut. The insect is trapped! Why do this plant and others like it need to trap insects? Find out on **pages 48-49** of **The World of Plants.**

## Story time

### Jack's beans

◆ When Jack sells the family cow for a handful of beans, his mother is furious. She throws the beans out the window. But the beans are magic. Turn to **pages 12-21** of **Once Upon a Time** and read what happens when the magic beans start to grow.

### A big pumpkin

◆ Pumpkins can grow to a fine size. But have you ever seen one big enough to live in? You can read about a huge pumpkin on **page 25** of **Poems and Rhymes.**

### Plants in danger

◆ When we think of endangered wildlife, we usually think of animals. But some plants are in danger, too. Can you help plants in danger? Read about the problem on **pages 168-175** of **The World of Plants.**

### A garden in a bottle

◆ You do not need a garden to grow your own plants. Try growing a tiny garden inside a glass jar or fish bowl. **Pages 128-129** of **The World of Plants** will show you how.

## Pressed flowers

◆ You can make lots of things with dried leaves and flowers, like a picture or a special gift card. **Pages 32-33** of **Art Around Us** tell you how to press flowers and leaves. Once you have a good collection, you can enjoy flowers and leaves all year around.

## Plant quiz

Here are some questions about plants. Try to think of the answers. Then turn to the pages listed to find the answers.

◆ What is a deciduous tree? **volume 5, page 36**

◆ What plants grow on the moon? **volume 7, page 54**

◆ Why don't we eat rhubarb leaves? **volume 5, page 44**

◆ What part do plants play in the food chain? **volume 4, page 162**

# The Sea

## The seas of the world

◆ Did you know that the land you live on is really just a big island with water all around it? Look at the view of the earth from space on **page 75** of **Our Earth.** All the blue parts are water. Almost three-quarters of the earth is covered with water. Do you know the names of the seas and oceans?

## Sea power

### Tides

◆ Imagine you are on a beach, and the sea is a long way down the beach from where you are standing. You go away. Then you come back after six hours, and the sea is close to you. What do you think has happened? Find out on **pages 58-59** of **The Universe.**

### Waves

◆ Have you ever stood on the beach and watched the waves rush in and out? Waves are very powerful. As they pound against the rocky shore, they crush rock into sand and shape the land. Read how this happens on **pages 80-83** of **Our Earth.**

### A wall of water

◆ A high wave called a tsunami can sweep over a shore in a wall that's 100 feet (30 meters) high. Read about what causes these huge waves on **page 77** of **Our Earth.**

## How do ships float?

◆ If you throw a stone into the sea, it will sink. A ship is made of heavy steel, so why doesn't it sink? If you turn to **pages 64-65** of **How Things Work,** you will find out.

## The ocean floor

◆ The bottom of the ocean has mountains that are taller and valleys that are longer and deeper than any on land. Get a look at the shape of the ocean floor on **pages 68-69** of **Our Earth**.

## Studying the sea

◆ How would you like to live under the sea? Scientists called oceanographers sometimes dive deep under the sea in special suits or in submarines. **Pages 100-101** of **Our Earth** describe what oceanographers study beneath the water.

## These rocks are alive!

◆ Coral is as hard as rock. But it is actually made of the skeletons of millions of tiny creatures called polyps. See how polyps cluster together to form all sorts of shapes on **pages 114-115** of **The World of Animals.**

## Sea greens

◆ They look like plants, but they're not. Read **pages 52-53** of **The World of Plants** to learn all about seaweeds and how they are perfectly suited for life in the ocean.

## Sea shells

◆ Do you ever pick up shells from the beach? There are lots of different shapes and sizes. Each shell once may have been the home of an animal called a mollusk. **Pages 110-111** of **The World of Animals** will tell you about life inside a shell.

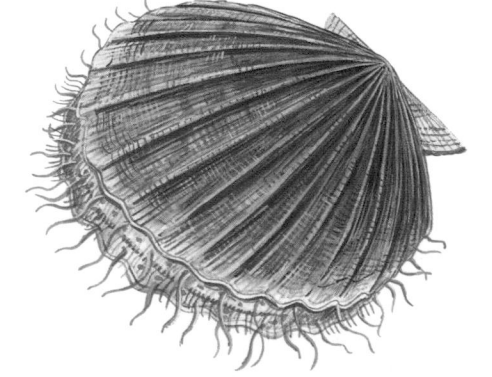

# Story time

### A promise kept
◆ Yukio, the son of a whale hunter, makes a promise to a whale stranded on the shore. Find out how he manages to keep his promise on **pages 180-189** of **Once Upon a Time**.

### Love at sea
◆ The owl and the pussycat sail away together in their pea-green boat, and before long they are married. Do you want to know if they lived happily ever after? Read **pages 130-131** of **Poems and Rhymes**.

### Going down . . .
◆ Imagine you are in a special ship deep down on the ocean bed. Hundreds of tons of water press down on you. Only the thick steel walls of your submarine protect you from being crushed. Want to know more? Turn to **pages 70-71** of **How Things Work**.

## Don't drink the water
◆ One thing you cannot get from the sea is a drink. If you did drink some seawater, you would be even thirstier. Why do you think this is? **Page 78** of **Our Earth** explains why.

## Traveling on the sea

### Ships galore!
◆ How many different kinds of ships can you think of? There are many ships to see on **pages 68-69** of **How Things Work**.

## Sea quiz

Here are some questions about the sea. Try to think of the answers. Then turn to the pages listed to find the answers.

◆ How many legs does a lobster have? **volume 4, page 140**

◆ What happens to a shark if it stops swimming? **volume 4, page 104**

◆ What is the name for a protected body of water? **volume 13, page 46**

◆ How is an island formed? **volume 6, page 56**

◆ Can you hear sound under water? **volume 8, page 144**

# The Sky

## What is the sky?

◆ Long ago, people believed that the sky was a roof stretched over the earth! But do you know what the sky is? Find out on **pages 104-105** of **Our Earth.**

## Bridges in the sky

◆ Have you ever tried to find the end of a rainbow? People once believed that a pot of gold was buried there. Other people thought that a rainbow was a bridge that appeared in the sky when the gods wanted to visit the earth. **Pages 138-139** of **Our Earth** explain what rainbows really are.

## Shapes in the sky

◆ Are there clouds in the sky today? What shape are they? Sometimes clouds look like big blobs of ice cream, and sometimes they look like wispy, floating feathers. There are many different kinds of clouds, and each kind has a name. You can learn some different names of clouds on **pages 126-127** of **Our Earth.**

## Danger from above

### Storms

◆ Tornadoes, hurricanes, whirlwinds, and twisters. These are all names for terrible storms. But where do the storms come from? Read **pages 120-123** of **Our Earth.**

### Acid rain

◆ In northern Europe, some of the forest trees are dying. The fish and small animals living near lakes and rivers are dying, too. Acid rain is polluting the land and water. Why does the rain become acid rain? **Pages 174-175** of **The World of Plants** describe what happens.

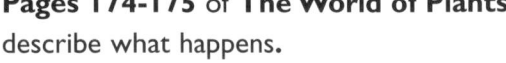

## Stars in the sky

◆ Look up at the sky on a clear night. You may be able to see thousands of twinkling stars scattered all over the sky. Sometimes the stars make shapes and patterns. One pattern looks like a great bear. Another looks like a dragon. All these patterns, and the stars in them, have names. You can find out what some are called and how to find them on **pages 108-109** and **114-117** of **The Universe.**

## Using the sun

◆ Long ago, there were no clocks or watches. People could only guess the time of day by seeing where the sun was in the sky. Another early way to tell the time was to use shadows. Some of the first clocks were shadow clocks and sundials. You can make your own sundial. **Page 175** of **Shapes and Numbers** explains how.

## Make a simple telescope

◆ Hans Lippershey, a Dutch maker of eyeglasses, made the first telescope in 1608. He put two lenses with slightly different shapes at opposite ends of a tube. The following year, Galileo Galilei, an Italian scientist, made his own telescope after hearing about the work of Lippershey. Galileo was one of the first people to use the telescope to look at things in the sky. You can make a simple telescope using two mirrors and a magnifying glass. For directions, look on **pages 148-149** of **The Universe.**

## The wind blows

◆ The wind bends the treetops and ruffles your hair. It drives the sails of a windmill and blows yachts on the sea. Wind is moving air. But why does the air move? Find out on **pages 112-113** of **Our Earth.**

## Flying in the sky

◆ All birds have wings, and most birds use their wings to fly. You can learn how birds fly on **pages 58-59** of **The World of Animals.**

## Our neighbor

◆ The stars are thousands of millions of miles away. The sun is the star nearest to our planet. But the moon is our nearest neighbor. How far away do you think the moon is? Look on **page 41** of **The Universe.**

## Flying machines

### Jets

◆ The engines hum, and the aircraft starts to move. A great roar fills the air as powerful jets drive you faster and faster down the runway. What happens next? **Pages 74-75** of **How Things Work** will give you the answer.

### Helicopters

◆ With its whirling blades, a helicopter can move in ways that an airplane cannot. What special jobs is this flying machine good for? Find out on **pages 72-73** of **How Things Work.**

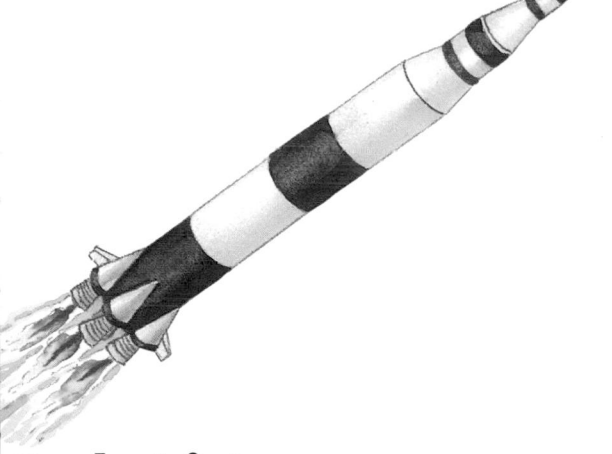

## The auroras

◆ Shimmering, glowing colors fill the sky on a cold, polar night. What a treat for the eyes! Even though it's nighttime, these colors are caused by the sun. Are you interested in how this happens? Then turn to **pages 136-137** of **The Universe.**

## Sky quiz

Here are some questions about the sky. Try to think of the answers. Then turn to the pages listed to find the answers.

◆ What is the name of the machine that helps pilots know where they are flying? **volume 9, page 94**

◆ How fast can the Concorde jet fly? **volume 13, page 55**

◆ What ancient people flew kites? **volume 12, page 104**

◆ What is the Milky Way made of? **volume 7, page 128**

◆ What are the only mammals that can fly? **volume 4, page 42**

◆ How can we store the power of wind? **volume 8, page 68**

## Rocket into space

◆ If you want to fly to the moon and back, you need a very big rocket. The Saturn V moon rocket burned three tons of fuel each second. Find out how rockets are launched on **pages 78-79** of **How Things Work.**

## Helpers in orbit

◆ Out in space, there are many artificial satellites. They circle the earth, doing many different jobs. They may be watching the weather or beaming radio messages from one country to another. Read **pages 104-105** of **How Things Work** to find out more about how satellites work. **Pages 44-45** of **How Does It Happen?** explain why satellites stay in orbit around the earth instead of flying off into space.

# The Animal Kingdom

## Meet the animals

### Mammals

◆ Do you have a pet mammal? If you have a dog, a cat, or a rabbit, then you do. Find out how you are like your pet mammal on **pages 32-33** of **The World of Animals.**

### Reptiles and amphibians

◆ Slimy, slippery, scaly, or smooth—is it a reptile or an amphibian? Get to know how to tell these creepy-crawly creatures apart on **pages 68-69** and **82-83** of **The World of Animals.**

### Birds

◆ Birds come in many shapes and sizes. Some storks grow to 5 feet (1.5 meters) tall. A bee hummingbird is hardly as long as your thumbnail. But all birds have one thing in common that makes them different from all other animals. Find out what that is on **pages 50-51** of **The World of Animals.**

### Animals without backbones

◆ From cockroaches to clams, spiders to sea urchins, this large group of animals has one thing in common—none of them has a backbone. What are these many kinds of animals called? **Pages 108-109** of **The World of Animals** will tell you.

## Animal remains

◆ Have you ever looked for fossils? If you are lucky and look really hard, you may find a piece of an ancient animal. **Pages 36-37** of **Our Earth** tell you how animals turn into fossils.

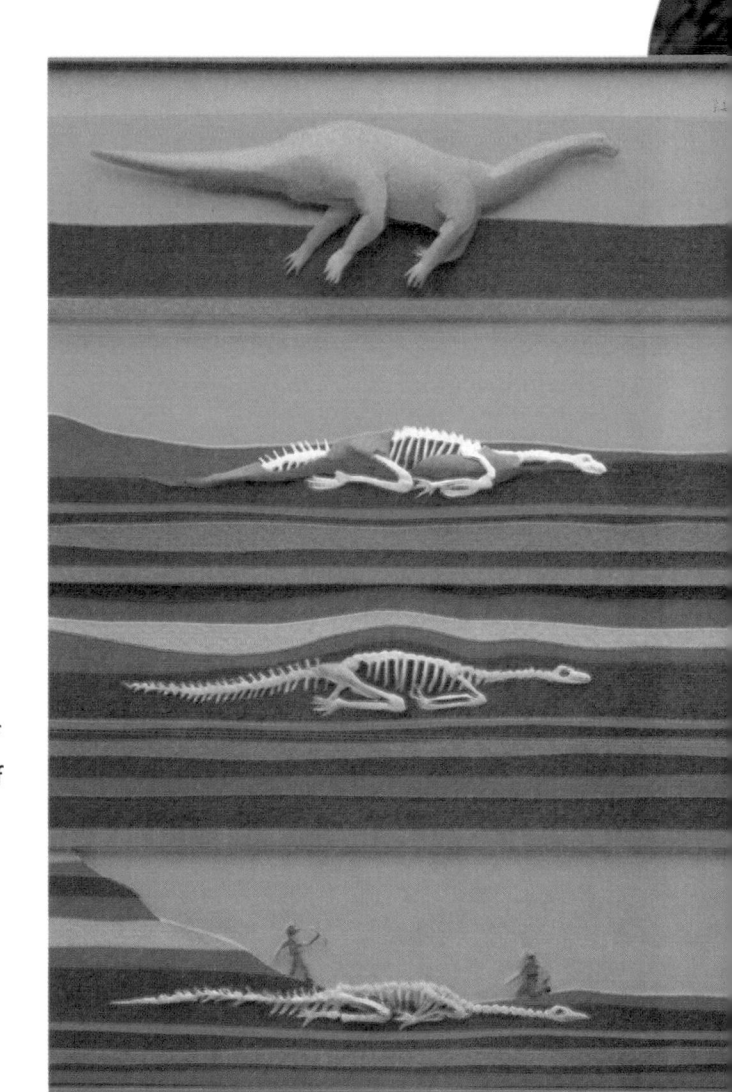

## Animals in danger

◆ Have you ever seen a dodo? Well, no, you could not have seen one, because they are all dead. But you can see a picture of one on **page 167** of **The World of Animals.** Many other kinds of animals that used to live in the world have now died out. Could this happen to any of the animals alive today? Yes, it could. Find out about some of the animals in danger on **pages 178-179** of **The World of Animals.**

## Bathe a buffalo

◆ Have you ever bathed a buffalo? Probably not. But some children in Asia take their family's buffaloes to be bathed. You can find out why the buffaloes need a bath on **pages 168-169** of **Who We Are.**

## Animal magic

◆ Why would an insect look like a twig? Find out and get to know some other animals that are not what they seem on **pages 148-149** of **The World of Animals.**

## Story time

### A brave coyote

◆ Native Americans tell a story of how the coyote helped the people when their world was dark and cold. Find out what the brave coyote did by reading the story on **pages 104-111** of **How Does It Happen?**

## Why is it so?

◆ Do you know why the bear has a stumpy tail or why mosquitoes buzz in people's ears? Read the stories on **pages 106-107** and on **pages 108-117** of **Once Upon a Time** for some make-believe answers!

## Animal quiz

Here are some questions about animals. Try think of the answers. Then turn to the pages listed to find the answers.

◆ What were the names of two famous animal space travelers? **volume 7, page 164**

◆ How does a snake swallow its food? **volume 4, page 74**

◆ In which country do people drink reindeer's milk? **volume 12, page 50**

◆ Where does a baby koala live? **volume 4, page 36**

◆ How do birds and insects help plants? **volume 5, page 26**

# Traveling to Other Lands

## At school in other lands

◆ Do you go to the same school every day? Some children don't. They go to lots of different schools. Some days, they don't go to one at all! You can find out about the different ways the world's children go to school if you read **pages 118-123** of **Who We Are.**

## Houseboats and skyscrapers

◆ Houses are different all over the world. In dry places, some houses are built from mud or clay. Near water, people may live on houseboats. Find out how homes around the world are different—and how they are the same—on **pages 80-81** of **See the World.**

## A walk in the garden

◆ Wherever you may travel, you will find gardens. People all over the world like gardens, and they have created many different kinds. See some gardens from around the world on **pages 156-157** of **The World of Plants.**

## A pretend trip

◆ You don't have to hop on a plane to have an adventure in a distant land. All you need are a few books, some souvenirs, and a little imagination. Read how one boy saw Kenya, Japan, and Brazil without ever leaving his grandmother's house on **pages 64-69** of **See the World.**

## Blast off to Mars

◆ When people want to move to a new place, they don't have to worry about whether there is enough air there—unless they want to move to Mars! You can read all about what scientists think about sending people to Mars on **pages 78-79** of **The Universe.**

## Hello!

◆ If you traveled to another land, would you know how to say "hello"? **Pages 130-131** of **Who We Are** has seven ways of saying hello. To learn how to say "goodbye"—and more—in many languages, see **pages 30-31** of **See the World.**

## Let your body do the talking...

◆ ...but know what it is saying! When you clap your hands in Nigeria, what are you saying? When you nod your head in Bulgaria, are you sure you are saying "yes"? **Pages 134-137** of **Who We Are** will tell you.

## A rainbow world

◆ Pale with freckles, warm and brown, or dark—these are just a few of the beautiful shades of people's skin. On **pages 20-21** of **About You**, you can find out why people come in so many different colors.

# What day is it?

◆ The Chinese calendar follows the moon, and each year is named for an animal. The Hebrew year may be 353 days short or 385 days long. Find out about these world calendars on **pages 16-19** of **Celebrate!**

# Traveling to other lands quiz

Here are some questions about traveling to other lands. Try to think of the answers. Then turn to the pages listed to find the answers.

◆ What continent is also a country? **volume 13, page 24**

◆ Is the equator a line of latitude or longitude? **volume 13, page 152**

◆ What travels at 186,282 miles (299,792 kilometers) per second? **volume 7, page 14**

◆ What is the name of the network that links computers all over the world? **volume 9, page 106**

◆ What kind of orchestra might you hear in Indonesia? **volume 3, page 110**

# Puppets

◆ Dancing on strings or floating on sticks, puppets move in many ways. Visit some of the world's puppets on **pages 166-169** of **Art Around Us.**

# Making memories

◆ If you are a world traveler, you will probably want to remember all the places you have seen. **Pages 174-175** of **See the World** are full of good ideas for keeping those memories alive.

# Food and Drink

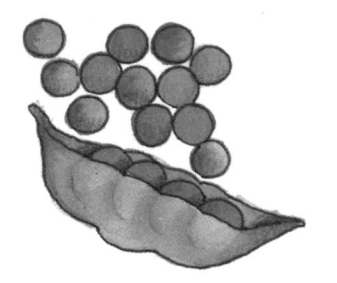

## Why do we eat?

◆ Your body is like a machine. Like a car, it needs fuel to keep it going. But instead of gasoline, you use food. Food gives you energy to help you grow. Do you know which foods make your body work best? Find out about healthy eating on **pages 160-163** of **About You.**

## All kinds of food

### Meat

◆ If you eat meat, then you probably eat some beef, pork, lamb, and chicken. Which kind of meat do you eat most? There are lots of reasons why people eat some kinds of meat more than other kinds. Read about them on **pages 56-57** of **Who We Are.**

### Vegetables

◆ Did you eat roots for dinner? Or seeds? You may have, but you probably did not use those names. Carrots and potatoes are the roots of plants, and beans are seeds. Can you think of any other parts of plants that people eat as food? Look at **pages 94-97** of **The World of Plants** for other examples.

### Bread

◆ Baguette, pita, chapatti, tortilla—these are all names for the kinds of bread you can eat around the world. See what shapes and sizes they are on **pages 46-47** of **Who We Are.**

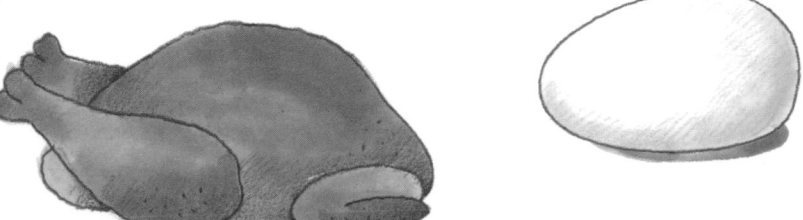

## Milk drinkers

◆ Many people drink milk that comes from cows. But many other kinds of animals give milk. Can you guess which animals people get their milk from in Greece, Saudi Arabia, and Tibet? Check your answers on **pages 50-51** of **Who We Are.**

## Far-out food

◆ Astronaut food has come a long way since people first started to explore space. Find out what today's space travelers munch on, on **Page 176** of **The Universe.**

## Rice for a hungry world

◆ Rice is served at every meal by more than half the world's people. Find out why rice is so important on **pages 48-49** of **Who We Are.**

## A good harvest

◆ For thousands of years, people have held celebrations to mark the gathering of crops in the fall. Food was plentiful, so people gave thanks and feasted. Read about harvest feasts on **pages 145, 168-169,** and **182** of **Celebrate!**

## Story time

◆ Dad's pudding was so good, young Huey and Julian couldn't resist. They ate it all up. Read all about their punishment on **pages 166-177** of **Once Upon a Time.**

## Stewing and sizzling

◆ There are many different ways of cooking food. In China, the food might be stir-fried in a little hot oil in a big, round-bottomed metal pan called a wok. How many other ways of cooking can you think of? You may find some you haven't thought of on **pages 60-61** of **Who We Are.**

## Cook something

◆ Give someone special a treat and fix them a really healthful breakfast or snack. You will find recipes for a breakfast sundae and snack kabobs on **pages 164-167** of **About You.**

## Your stomach at work

◆ *Munch, munch, munch.* You have just eaten your favorite food. But have you ever wondered what happens to your food once you have swallowed it? When it is inside your body, your food makes an incredible journey. **Pages 52-55** of **About You** describe how far your food travels.

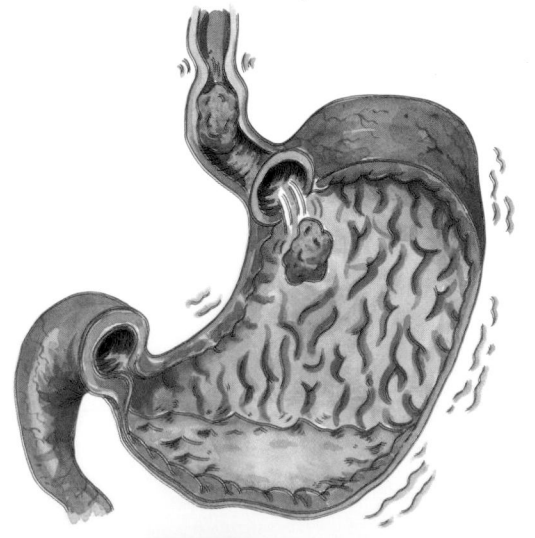

## Food and drink quiz

Here are some questions about food and drink. Try to think of the answers. Then turn to the pages listed to find the answers.

◆ What do Muslims eat in the daytime during Ramadan? **volume 14, page 30**

◆ In which countries do people eat with chopsticks? **volume 12, page 66**

◆ What do you call an animal that eats only plants? **volume 4, page 12**

◆ What kind of energy does food contain? **volume 8, page 78**

◆ What is added to milk to make it harden into cheese? **volume 9, page 122**

# Large and Small

## The biggest...

### Mountain

◆ The top of Mount Everest is the highest place in the world. Mount Everest stands between Tibet and Nepal in Asia. Find out how mountains form and how they are worn away on **pages 50-53** of **Our Earth.**

### Planet

◆ Jupiter is the biggest planet in our solar system. It would take more than 1,000 Earths to fill Jupiter. But it wouldn't be a very good place to live. **Page 81** of **The Universe** will tell you why.

## Animals

◆ Everybody knows that animals come in all sizes, but do you know which animals are the biggest? Find out which are the smallest, too, on **pages 144-145** of **The World of Animals.**

### Plant

◆ This tree grows as tall as a 37-story building. Find out what it is on **pages 38-39** of **The World of Plants.**

### Number

◆ What's the biggest number there is? Is it a million? No. Is it a googol? Check **pages 106-107** of **Shapes and Numbers** to find out.

## The smallest...

### Planet

◆ In the sun's family, there are small planets called asteroids. Find out on **pages 96-97** of **The Universe** what happens when they collide with other planets.

### Things

◆ Do you know what you are made of? Billions and billions of tiny atoms. They are far too small to see. Read **pages 74-75** of **How Does It Happen?** to find out what happens when an atom is split in two.

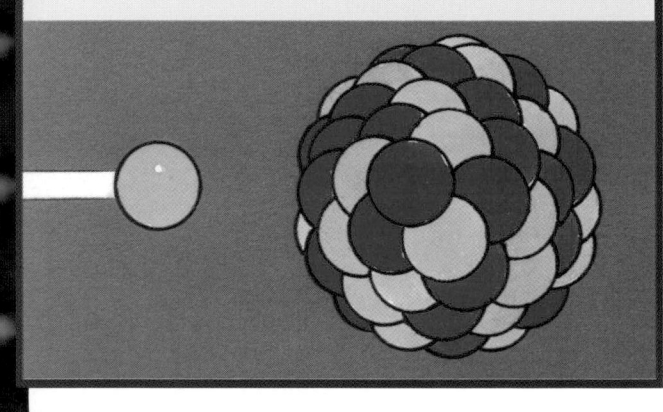

## Growing up

◆ Every person in the world began life as a tiny egg inside the mother's body. That tiny egg grew into a baby, and then was born. A baby goes on growing until it is an adult, just as you will. Think how much that tiny egg has grown! See how an egg grows on **pages 92-93** of **About You.**

## Families large and small

◆ There are many kinds of families in the world. The smallest family has just one child and one parent. But families can be much bigger. How many people are there in your family? Find out about other families on **pages 10-13** of **Who We Are.**

## Story time

◆ One day, a lion decided not to eat a little mouse. In return, the mouse promised to help the lion. How could a little mouse help a huge lion? Read **page 171** of **Poems and Rhymes.**

## Close-ups

◆ Have you ever looked at your hand through a magnifying glass? It makes your hand look much bigger. If you look through a telescope, you can see much farther than your hand. But how do these magnifiers work? Look on **pages 122-123** of **How Does It Happen?** and **pages 146-147** of **The Universe.**

## Into the distance

◆ Artists use certain ways of drawing to make us think that we can see into the distance in their pictures. One way is to draw everything close to the front of the picture much larger than the things far away at the back. **Pages 58-59** of **Art Around Us** will show you some other ways to do this.

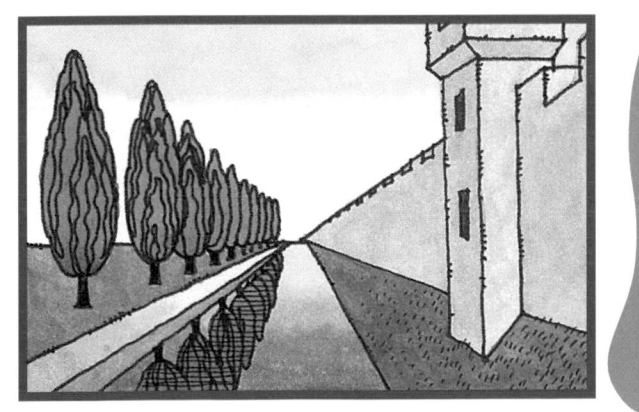

## A land for little people

◆ Imagine that you are 165 feet (50 meters) tall. You would tower above the trees and buildings. There is a city in the Netherlands where you would be just like that! Everything in the city of Madurodam is 25 times smaller than real life. See a picture of this mini-town on **page 97** of **Art Around Us.**

## Large and small quiz

Here are some questions about large and small. Try to think of the answers. Then turn to the pages listed to find the answers.

◆ How many moons travel around the giant planet Jupiter? **volume 7, page 80**

◆ What are the tiny blood cells that help cuts heal? **volume 11, page 48**

◆ What is the giant statue in Egypt's desert called? **volume 3, page 90**

◆ Where is the world's longest wall? **volume 13, page 105**

◆ Where is the Giant's Causeway? **volume 6, page 28**

# Machines

## Machines are for moving!

### Levers

◆ Can you lift your best friend above your head? It doesn't sound easy, but it is. If you and your friend sit on a seesaw, that's exactly what you are doing. Read **pages 10-11** of **How Does It Happen?** to find out what makes it easy.

### Pulleys

◆ A hippo is heavy, that's for sure. But with a very simple machine—and lots of rope—you and a friend could lift one. You don't believe it? Just turn to **pages 22-23** of **How Does It Happen?**

## Muscle machines

◆ Did you know that your own body is a machine? It is made of bones that fit together at joints. Muscles move you by pushing and pulling on your bones. You can see how bones and muscles work together on **pages 44-45** of **About You.**

## A picker-upper

◆ The alligator machine on **pages 12-13** of **How Does It Happen?** can help you pick up things you can't quite reach. And you can make it yourself!

### Wheels

◆ Imagine a world in which there are no wheels. There would be no cars, no trucks, and no bicycles. How would you carry things from one place to another? How do wheels help? Read **pages 20-21** of **How Does It Happen?**

## Robots in action

◆ With a click and a whirl, the shining machine trundles around the workshop. It is a robot, and it is helping to build a car. How does it know what to do? Find out on **pages 174-175** of **How Things Work.**

## Move yourself!

◆ Sit on a bicycle with your feet on the pedals. Push once with one foot, then with the other. How far have you traveled? You have moved much farther than if you had taken two steps forward. If you can't figure out why, read **pages 50-51** of **How Things Work.**

## A machine that never stops?

◆ Dr. Mothbold has built an automatic polka-dotting machine. "My machine will never stop!" he says proudly. Is he right or is he wrong? Look on **pages 36-37** of **How Does It Happen?** to find out.

## Cars and carburetors

◆ Look at the cars going down the street. There are many different shapes and sizes. But most of them work in the same way. Do you know what makes a car move? Look at **pages 54-57** of **How Things Work.**

## Poison in the air

◆ Machines don't always help us. Before factories and cars were invented, the air was much cleaner. Today, smoke and fumes damage trees, soil, and rivers. Pollution from factories also can kill fish and land animals. It even can heat up the earth. **Pages 164-165** and **168-169** of **Our Earth** describe how this happens.

## Machines in the home

### A washing machine

◆ Dirty clothes? Put them in the washing machine. How hard do you want them to twist and tumble? How hot do you want the water? Tell your machine, and then it does all the work. Find out how on **pages 20-21** of **How Things Work.**

### Television

◆ What's on TV tonight? Thousands of lines filled with light! **Pages 88-89** of **How Things Work** describe how a TV picture is formed. Want to change channels? You can read how a remote control works on **pages 92-93** of **How Things Work.**

## Music machines

◆ Press a key and you hear a note. Have you ever wondered what's inside those machines we call keyboards? Read all about them on **pages 122-123** of **Art Around Us.**

## Machines quiz

Here are some questions about machines. Try to think of the answers. Then turn to the pages listed to find the answers.

◆ What happens when you press the button on a camera? **volume 8, page 126**

◆ What is a fulcrum? **volume 8, page 10**

◆ What is the name of a counting machine made with beads and wires? **volume 10, page 54**

◆ What is the name of the spinning wheel that moves a jet aircraft? **volume 9, page 74**